The Black Man's Guide to Self-Improvement Post-Pandemic

Alright Black Man, Where Do We Go from Here?

(D. Forte)

(Alright, Black Man Where Do We Go from Here)
Copyright © 2021 by (D. Nathaniel)

All rights reserved. No part of this book may be reproduced or transmitted in any form or by any means without written permission from the author.

ISBN (978-0-578-81860-3)

Printed in USA

This book is a guide for Black Men to place into perspective the importance and significance of the time that we are living in presently. Overall, the book is about self-improvement for men which the principles in this guide should be used to better ourselves and our communities. Presented in this book is honest conversation and tangible solutions related to the positive pathways for Black Male Masculinity. The ultimate goal of this book is to teach and re-affirm in Black Men the ways in which to build/uplift ourselves and the community. I genuinely believe this is our life's mission and the purpose that the Most-High intended for us to follow.

Dedication

To the Most-High to whom without Him nothing would be possible. To all the great Black men past and present that have shown us the way so that we would not be within the wilderness without guidance. To the journey of self-improvement, so that whenever the Most High brings about the day that none of us no longer exist on this Earth, may our lives have served as a light to other Brothers who may be in the midst of the storm or challenges that may arise in life.

Preface

This book was written as a result of an unprecedented pandemic, social injustices, pain within our community that has not ceased, and the ultimate lack of sovereignty that we as Black Men must have to be the leaders of our community (we as Black Men must have sovereignty and lead with sovereignty in our individual lives).

I personally do not know what happened, but partially we have lost our way within our communities. We have allowed lawlessness, selfishness, ungodliness, self-hatred, pain, defeat, and lack of guardianship run rampant through our communities.

Yet, because of a global pandemic that has occurred for the first time in our lifetime and quite possible for the last time within duration of this jagged society, we have had time to sit still. The lack of access to daily norms and activities allowed time for us to reset, regroup, and retrain.

It is my hope, pray, and goal that we make it out of this time period as forever changed men with the intent to build better our communities. I believe the Most High gave us time to see what we will do (out of grace and mercy). Because our community and society as a whole is being swallowed up within the hands of wickedness as we speak (and I am not saying this out of fear but simply out of truth and wisdom). Thus, particularly this time post-pandemic is ushering in something different and I am not quite sure what it is exactly.

But we must be ready. What I do know is that I personally believe this is our final chance to get right and fix the community. The Most-High is allowing us one more time, chance, and opportunity to build our ark before the flood. He is searching far and wide for the righteous men of good faith and character.

If we do not fix our communities, heal our people, and build ourselves up as Black Men, I personally believe we will not get another chance. Society, sin, and the hurt of our community will be too great to overcome without a complete reboot. And this pandemic has given us the closest thing to that reboot, restart, reset (to the original setting). Black Man, we must take advantage of that opportunity.

That is why this book was created and developed. To offer a simple guide with hope, direction, and information so that we can change our communities for the better.

Introduction

To simply put it this book is a short guide and a simple resource for us to reset ourselves and our communities. We always hear about the issues, yet many never place the same energy within the solutions. Ultimately, the information listed will not completely change everything wrong within society and the pain that plaques many of our communities. Moreover, the information discussed will look different for each person (and each person must make individual decisions that are best for them). Yet, the book is a good place to start and begin to offer immediate ways to improve and elevate better outcomes.

This book is meant to offer solutions, invoke thought, and awaken Black Men so that we may begin to be the men that the Most High created us to be at all times. Being a man, particularly a Black Man of distinct character and substance is a way of life (and not just a singular thought or action).

Health

Health is extremely important; I am sure you heard the phrase "health is wealth." Heck, the statement is so much more important especially with everything that has happened in relation to the pandemic and all the changes that will take place post Covid.

It seems as if within this society, we have made bad health a good choice. We lust after and gluttonize fast-food, cheap opportunities, and instant glorification (physically, mentally, diet-wise, and other aspects).

I personally do not believe statistics at times tell the full story, but for this instance I will address the stats related to health. Black Men are at times statistically one of the last groups to see a doctor, and we as men in general are least likely to eat a highly concentrated green or evenly balanced diet in comparison to our counterparts. Additionally, we are more likely to be targets of stress which like many other factors socially and biologically; stress is a killer. Overall, Black Men are least likely to seek out self-care outlets and we face numerous other "stigmas" within the Black community that can jeopardize our health.

When I state this information, I personally don't mean the entire collective of Black Men. Thankfully, many of us have driven into the healthier lifestyles of balanced nutrition, constant exercise (strength training and cardio), and removing unhealthy foods from your daily diet (moderation is fine, but every day is detrimental).

But there is still a long way to go. Something that I have observed that is very troubling is the number of communities that are food deserts (meaning a viable healthy food option whether a grocery store or other outlet is not within reasonable walking or driving distance). Studies show that food deserts particularly within communities of color play a tremendous role within the poor health and dietary choices of certain communities.

Another thing that I see is a glorification of unhealthy foods. Within many communities of color where the intersection of race and socioeconomics are prevalent, we see the elements of poor health choices (generally from a lack of options or despair). Growing up, I took notice of my surroundings and what I saw in other communities. I saw (and still see) within many of our neighborhood are these three things: a raggedy gas station/corner store with poor food options, liquor stores, and deep-fried restaurants (the fried wing station, fried fish and things, deep fired express, fast food outlet, fired gizzards palace, heart disease empire, the house of gout, etc.).

I know it sounds crazy but tell me that I am wrong. Especially those who grew up in these very neighborhoods that I spent my life. The lack of healthy choices is not only marketed to us but normalized to the extent of no further options being offered in the very places that need them the most.

Now I love lemon-pepper wings and fried fish like the next person (but in moderation). But we must understand Black Man that there is no nutritional value in a plate of deep-fried wings and a container of French fries. As a matter of fact, many of the parts of the animals we eat are probably some of the dirtiest parts of the animal to eat.

Yet, we are mass marketed and routinely offered only this option of eating. We are constantly given this idea, and what happens. The same health issues that were addressed earlier ultimately become a cycle. Moreover, our diets will greatly affect us as we get older because ultimately the actions of our younger selves can either increase or decrease our risk for stroke, heart disease, diabetes, or other health issues.

In addition, we previously did not see a lot of gyms within our communities and even places to obtain vitamins or natural supplements (at least not the way we are starting to see them presently). Therefore, I want to say it is extremely important for us to adopt good health behaviors even despite the obstacles presented that attempt to block us from optimal health. And it is my hope that good habits will turn into healthy lifestyles (meaning a lifelong commitment to good health).

All in all, we need to correct our health and correct the health of our community. We see this process beginning to come into fruition slowly.

We are seeing the rise of community gardens and community farmers markets, which is great. But we need a lot more opportunities to access clean and fresh food which equates to better diets. Ultimately, better diets and better health behaviors equal healthier lifestyles. Everyone's diet and nutritional needs will be different per individual person, so the exact answer of how to improve your health can only be fully answered by you. But we can move towards a healthier lifestyle by adapting healthy behaviors and taking our health seriously as we serve within the role of protectors, providers, and men of purpose. Therefore, eat right and hit those weights.

Mental Health

If the circumstances surrounding Covid-19 have not taught us anything, one thing it has shown us is the importance of optimal mental health. Personally, the pandemic has been a wakeup call for many of us. Pay close attention and reflect for a moment. Everything that we loved and even the things we enjoyed were temporarily taken away from us at some point during this pandemic (sports, certain foods, hangout spots, non-essential work-related activities, the gym, the barbershop for Christ sake, and many other places/pillars of the community).

Within this pandemic, everything that we took refuge within previously and used to mask our misfortunates or conceal our conditions were temporarily taken away. Unless you live with your family or significant other, the pandemic caused you to be within the resting arms of solitude. It caused you to have to confront some of the things (emotions, ideas, or thoughts) that you could previously escape using temporary moments of ecstasy (or the scientific definition…dopamine).

Yet, the closure of numerous outlets caused us to have to rely heavily upon ourselves. For some that meant that emotions that were hidden deep inside of us came out (depression, anxiety, unhappiness, maybe even painful realization of not living life to the fullest). For others, the pandemic only magnified some of our problems, and some of the issues that were already weighing heavy upon us.

Statistically, Black Men are one of the least likely to seek out mental health or self-care resources. Many of us think that if we just throw our emotions or pain aside then eventually, they will subside (myself included at a certain point in my life). But stress, burdens, feelings related to past abandonment issues, or other pressures that try to disturb our peace will eventually show up whether we believe so or not.

I learned about self-care in college, and it changed my life. After researching the importance of self-care and taking advantage of a Black male emotional well-being (group discussion based) program on my campus, I started understanding why talking through the pressures of life was important. My thoughts regarding mental health and talking to someone instantly changed. I share my story with you because I hope it serves as a light to show the importance of self-care and that taking care of your mental health does not make you soft or unmanly.

It is the total opposite, we as men should be strong enough and focused enough to see a problem and have the honor as well as humility to attempt to fix that problem before it becomes an issue down the road.

We as Black Men must deal with a lot of things within ourselves, the community, and society in general. And each section at times cause slight cuts into our armor, but a good solider gets his armor inspected and repaired when needed.

There is great stigma within the Black community regarding mental health and counseling. Again, I was one of those guys and so were my friends until we grew up and learned better. It is a blessing that the maturation process regarding that topic happened as soon as it did for me. Some Black Men go through their entire life suffering in silence.

Not having an outlet to vent or a safe space to voice issues in life is difficult. Therefore, finding those spaces are particularly important, especially in these times. I wish many more places like the barbershop for Black Men would create events or times to have community discussions on mental health.

There has always been a level of mistrust and natural reservation when it comes to discussing ways to improve mental well-being. However, like picking the right barbershop, church, or gym…the path towards finding the best way to overcome emotional barriers and other factors that may affect you is about finding the best fit.

I understand that notion, and I am candidly honest that I do not share my inner thoughts with everyone. But finding a good Black counselor can help if needed. Some colleges offer counseling for free, certain jobs offer insurance that covers counseling, and there are several other avenues as well (therapyforblackmen.org for example). Either way, it is good to consider finding ways to take your overall health in every aspect seriously.

For many of us, the pandemic allowed time to be honest with ourselves and hopefully confront the emotions buried inside of us. This is done so that we can grow as men, and eventually grow as fathers, husbands, friends, mentors, leaders, and warriors. I think more than ever Covid has taught us that we can only control the things that we can control. For me, one of the things I can do better is learning to adapt and take control of my health as well as happiness. I can control those things by confronting raw emotions and learning to heal previous hurt, eating better, and taking responsibility for my overall health.

If given the opportunity, I would greatly advocate that Black Men who need it seek out Black counselors (those that are honest, certified, self-aware, and understanding of the issues facing Black Men). It is much better to seek out help then to seek out vices. Ultimately vices and instant ecstasy/gratification become addictive. And those addictions do not help ease the pain but only place on a thin layer of paint on a house that needs to be remodeled from the inside-out.

Therefore, bump the stigma. If needed, seek help and talk to someone you trust. To simply put it…seek health, heal past trauma, remove confusion from your life, separate yourself from toxic environments or relationships, and in-turn realign your life to the path of the Most-High (walking in righteousness, freedom, less burdens, abundance, and joy).

Education

Another thing that I know for sure this pandemic has taught us is the importance of education and educational versatility. When I say education, I mean within multiple forms and ideas. During the pandemic, we saw something we had never seen before which was a dividing line regarding jobs and opportunities (i.e., essential workers and non-essential workers).

The term essential and non-essential workers (which were terms that I heard for the first time ever in my lifetime) placed emphasis on the importance of job security and educational versatility. Although I believe that everyone and every job is essential within some basis, the terms draw a harsh conclusion. For me that conclusion was that the statement "only the strong survive" is limited to an extent. But the statement should be "only the strong and those that are adaptive/versatile shall survive."

Yet, the key to versatility is a good education. Now, education looks slightly different for everyone. For some that might be a bachelor's degree, JD, vocational certificate, or apprenticeship which then leads to a license within a particular career field. But whichever path you decide the basis of having a solid foundation should be based upon education/training.

During the pandemic, I took a sharper look at the fields that they considered to be essential thus lacking in some of the massive furloughs or job reductions. The essential jobs were construction, engineering, electricians, plumbers, H-VAC techs, lawyers, government employees, doctors, nurses, medical staff, police, security, grocery industry, logistics, warehouse workers, auto repair, robotics, computer science, cyber security, law enforcement, cleaning services, finance, banking, maintenance, mental health, social services, machinery, real estate, delivery services, and STEM jobs.

Yet, the key to all these fields is education (or a willingness to learn) and certifications to be an eligible professional within these areas. During this pandemic and even after the pandemic is over, you will have two types of people. Those that see and understand the trends, thus moving toward seeking education within the various fields mention. Or, at the very least become more diverse and versatile within the jobs that they currently work. Therefore, education should be key to transforming and continuing to be "essential."

Having multiple streams of income (which I will address later) and creating new lanes for yourself is extremely important. For example, the great A.G. Gaston (one of the greatest Black business owners of all-time) once said "find a need and fill it." He himself did just that which lead to him being a business titan within multiple areas (which I consider him to be the greatest entrepreneur of all-time in my opinion).

For the first time in a long time there was a global emphasis upon education with many organizations offering training and education at a reduced or waived cost. Even if your job was not within the "essential list", the education opportunities provided during these times offered the opportunity to gain experience and education to help you move up the ladder or make the leap toward another career entirely.

Whatever you do, honestly you should strive to be the absolute best at that thing. So, I am asking that you begin to seek out opportunities post-pandemic. In the potential next months and years please seek education and other opportunities to develop yourself.

During this pandemic alone, I have been more productive than ever before because I understood the principle of education. I have completed two certifications, worked on writing two books, learned how to build websites, and I started graduate school (all during a pandemic). Why? You may ask...

Because I understand the importance of being versatile and being adaptive. Therefore, go learn that trade or pursue that innovative idea because the more options that you have the better you will be in any situation.

If I could offer any advice to my younger self, I would have told myself to pursue a trade or certificate immediately after high school and/or during my time in college. I would have advised myself to take time out to find the balance to learn a skill (wielding, barbering, automobile technician skills, military experience, and other things) so that I could have a more diverse educational and workforce skill set.

Entrepreneurship/Multiple Streams of Income

Another clear objective that the pandemic has brought out is the need for multiple streams of income. If you remember in the previous topic, I talked about the idea of essential and non-essential workers being mentioned during this pandemic. I personally do not like the idea nor the terms that were tossed around.

However, I realize that when I clock-in to whatever company I am working at for that day, I am trading in my time for pay. In other words, I am trading in my precious time (life, energy, life force, portion of my existence) for a mere fraction or morsel of pay. Which I am using my time, talent, and essence to further cement or bring forth someone else's idea. My last name is not Walton (Walmart), Cathy (Chick Fil-A), or Jones (Dallas Cowboys).

No matter where I "work"; I am helping someone else profit and live out their dream of "ownership." No matter what sector you work within whether public or private sector, you are still working to bring someone's else goals, policies, or ideologies to life. You may be helping people and love your job, but it still is within the framework of someone's ideas. And, you still have to walk a fine line of innovation versus subordination.

Meaning even if you have an idea to change the world whether that is a societal idea or something to change a particular industry that you work within ultimately the idea may get shot down because it does not "fit" into the ideas or plans of the company. And it is not right or wrong, it is just simple reality. It is never personal, it is just business. Therefore, I advise any man to start his own business endeavors.

Entrepreneurship is key because it provides a certain level of sovereignty. Moreover, you are paid for the work that you put in entirely, and not by a predesignated "wage."

Think about it, even if your idea saves the company millions or you can secure an amazing contract/deal, you are limited to only a small portion of the proceeds. Now again its nothing wrong with that notion because that is the way life works. Moreover, I am a huge proponent of having multiple jobs and multiple streams of income. I love the job that I have, so even though I have my own platform, I will probably always work because I love what I do. Therefore, I am not saying quit your job. Just always have options, and never be limited to one thing.

Moreover, many states including my home state is legally considered an "at-will state." Meaning they can fire you basically "at-will" without offering just reason or due warning of your termination in most instances. Personally, I do not want any person to have that kind of control or power over my life. Yet, if the possibility of being vulnerable to the loss of income is that fluid, it is extremely important to have multiple solid streams of income.

That includes starting your business and having legal side hustles (for some that may be YouTube, video editing, landscaping, barbering, real estate, writing books, public speaking, voice overs, designing/selling clothes, reselling thrift items online, security work, painting, life coaching, resume writing, trading stocks, etc.).

But having viable and solid incomes to fall forward upon is especially important for Black Men at any age. Moreover, you want to leave a legacy for your descendants. The rapper Royce 5'9 hit a line in a freestyle that's summarize something like "planting trees so that even my advanced seeds (children and future generations) can enjoy the shade."

That's ultimately what I want for all Black Men to be able to do within their lifetime. Create legacy and generation wealth so that may leave strong families (mentally, physically, spiritually, and financially).

Buying a Life Insurance Policy

Speaking of advance seeds enjoying the legacy left by you, it is important to prepare for the future. Eventually, we must all transition to the next life but before we do, I believe it is the responsibility of every brother to make sure his family is good.

When you think about it honestly, we know life is short. We all have a time clock, and when it runs out it just runs out. But we must be prepared for everything in life as men even the very end of our earthly existence. I believe that Dr. Boyce Watkins said it best when he said that "only the Black community has a tradition of leaving their family in debt when they die instead of leaving them with some form of wealth."

That is why I believe it is extremely important that every Black Man have an insurance policy. If this pandemic has not taught us anything, it has taught us just how unpredictable and fragile life can be at times.

Surprisingly, both aspects of being born and dying (at least within the traditional western societal formats) are not free, and they are not cheap either. Passing away will at least cost several grand when you include burial, plot, casket, and fees. Sounds weird to be discussing especially within this context, but we as Black Men cannot afford to run from reality.

Therefore, I believe it should be a requirement to buy life insurance and the good part is that the sooner the better, meaning the earlier you buy it the cheaper it is. There are several policy structures like term or whole life for example. Without getting too specific, a term life policy is a policy that you can buy which pays out if you transition within a certain time frame (you can buy a term policy with a ten-, twenty-, thirty-, or forty-year option).

In addition, if you want something a little more attractive regarding the perks of buying life insurance you can buy a whole life policy. Which means that the insurance policy accumulates a cash value that can be borrow or taken from before you transition (fees do apply, though) which you can use to purchase appreciating assets or cover unexpected expenses. In addition, the policy covers your entire life (meaning it has no term limitations).

Of course, whole life insurance may be more expensive depending upon the structure you choose, but it may also be more flexible and versatile. Before you make any decision about which path to take, I would always recommend doing research on finding which one is best for you before making the purchase. And you can always go through an insurance agent if you want a more personal experience then directly buying it online.

Sovereignty and Self-Sufficiency

Although, no one saw this pandemic coming…those that were more prepared for the unpredictable were a lot better off than those who were already struggling (or at the very least unprepared for the things that transpired- i.e., furloughs, lay-offs, limits on the amount of food we were able to purchase, stock market crashing, etc.).

Unfortunately for many of us that meant that we were scrambling if not prepared. Although the pandemic altered many of my plans and it hurt my wallet slightly, it honestly was not that bad. I do not mean that in an arrogant manner but laying out the importance of being prepared. Let me take it a step further and break it down.

I have been able to build upon great local leaders in my community and even a few great content creators from various media platforms that I have learned from over the last couple of years. One thing that I realized is the importance of a man building boundaries and sovereignty.

What I see in common with many success people is the quest for sovereignty. Again, I am not against working as I will always hold a job and multiple streams of income via various opportunities. But we as men cannot be sovereign unless we have something of our own that we control, and that we can build upon even if other avenues do not work for whatever reason (and within this case an unprecedented pandemic).

Therefore, as men we need to create opportunities to build diverse financial growth and streams of income. Overall, it may look different for each of us but being self-sufficient within yourself (and ultimately your family) is key. Building sovereignty is building a life that you can control and create outcomes that are beneficial to your life (and the lives of others).

Creating a Savings

Creating sovereignty is key to a successful life in more ways than one in my opinion. But just as important as creating self-sufficiency is also creating financially stability within the perspective of always being prepared. This pandemic has taught us that no time traveling sage will come personally knock on your door and tell you to get ready because a "storm is a coming." No, it does not work like that for most of us.

Experts say that it is imperative to have at least three months' worth of full expenses saved up as a good starting point for saving (in case of emergencies or unforeseen circumstances). Therefore, let us say that your rent, utilities, car payments (insurance and actual car notes), gas, food, vitamins, life insurance, and other expenses (and even some fun spending money) totals about 1600 per month.

Of course, it could be more or less depending upon your financial situation and overall lifestyle. But the sake of conversation let's say $1600 per month. That means that you need to save at the very least $4800 dollars in your saving account (and maybe even more as some expert says six months of living expenses should be saved up).

The $4800 hundred dollars is solely for short term and immediate expenses, which would be saved up for a rainy day. For some that figure is easy to save up for because they live below their means. For others it may be more difficult, heck most Americans regardless of race or gender do not have that kind of monthly income saved up. Statistically close to 50% (if not more) of people live paycheck to paycheck.

But if you break it down per month then it is actually not that hard. You can save the $4800 hundred in a year or less (less than a year if you save aggressively). If you break down the forty-eight hundred dollars down by twelve months, it's basically saving four hundred dollars per month (which is right around one hundred dollars per week).

Again, I don't know your financial situation but think about it like this right here. If you work a traditional Monday through Friday (8 to 5) job without any other weekend job opportunities, then it simply means picking up a weekend job (during the pandemic companies like Target, Walmart, Walgreens, Shipt, GrubHub, Doordash were hiring like crazy) that pays at least ten dollars per hour and working at minimum, ten hours per week (well actually more like twelve to fourteen hours because you must account for taxes).

Even if you already have a weekend job and cannot afford to save that money which you would allocate straight to a savings. You can even attempt to get an afternoon job to work immediately after you get off your 8am-5pm job. That is basically what I have been doing even before the pandemic hit. I work from 8am-5pm, then I go to my next job and get off around 10pm. And then, I work on the weekends faithfully.

Now, every man has a different path and even I plan my financial endeavors slightly different than most. Personally, I am not saying you got to get four different jobs. Moreover, the ultimate goal as AMS says in his best-selling book "Alpha Money Strategies" is to work for yourself, and not solely have to trade time for a set wage.

However, we are all doing what we have to do for right now to have the outcomes in the future that we want. Right now, I generally work two to three jobs because I know what I am trying to pursue in the end. But again, you must figure out what works best for your life. Yet, the consensus is building yourself up spiritually, mentally, physically, and financially to endure any storm that life may bring unexpectedly.

While waiting for that sovereignty and foundation to be built, it is my personal goal to try to work at least sixty hours per week (your plan might be slightly different depending on family needs and other responsibilities). I once heard a wise man say that every single man (with no otherwise outstanding responsibilities) should work at least sixty hours a week. Which for me is a full-time job and a constant part-time weekend job.

Moreover, there are several jobs that offer work from home options and other jobs that offer higher hourly wages to which the tailored number of hours may be different for you. But either way until you can build the situation that is best for you, then working and saving up is key.

Multiple Streams of Income

A major portion of this entire book has been about sovereignty and creating positive outcomes during unpredictable or unprecedented times. This is no different as I believe that having multiple streams of income is absolutely the only way to go in 2021 and beyond. Let's keep it one hundred, expenses are constantly going up. The cost of living is constantly increasing, and there is always this thing called "inflation" that comes around periodically to shrink money that is either "just sitting there" or has not increased with the times.

Having multiple streams of income is important because it is one of the keys to sovereignty (particularly the principle of wealth creation through business ownership and the almighty principle of passive income). Multiple streams can help create generational wealth, and at the bare minimum offer some comfort or degree of cushion if anything unexpected happens.

I understand that within these two principles that we must always be prepared as men. Moreover, we don't have the societal luxuries that others possess, so it is extremely imperative for us to have a plan A and at least a good plan B as well (but it cannot be built overnight because it takes time).

Having multiple streams of income, and multiple avenues of passive income is especially important. But like I mentioned in the previous topic having a savings is just as important. Multiple streams of income are nothing without financial literacy and discipline. The rapper fabulous said it best in the song ***Summer On Lock***

"You ain't got a hundred 'till you got two hundred, learn life. Respect ain't earned twice, once you lose it, it's gone. **And it's lame when your money right but you using it wrong**."

Brothers that is a bar for any aspect of life.

Buying Property

"Telling me longevity is in the dirt. Should buy some property first. Should profit a better dollar with generational perks. Equity at his best, really, you should invest. These tangible things expire, don't you expect. Income with so much outcome and yes. Look at my heritage, we blessed." – Kendrick Lamar "Multiply"

I think these lyrics by Kendrick Lamar offer great insight into the ideas and perspectives that each of us should have regarding the idea of property and ownership. It is sad that during the early post war America (and early as well as mid 1950s) due to unfair practices, misunderstanding or mistrust of proper land laws, discrimination, individual as well as systemic racism, and the lack of opportunities for loans or grants, Black people lost upwards to 80% of the farmland/property owned (some estimations say even more).

But just as the land was stripped away so was in many regards the ownership mindset. It instantly placed generations within the mindset of renting or a modified sharecropping mindset (working for the same system that owns the land just to make the same system rich while we receive little compensation for the labor which in turn is given back to us as tenants of property that we probably paid for ten times over).

I believe it is important for us as Black people to have an ownership mindset when it comes to business, property, and other aspects of life. Buying unnecessary things that don't equate to financial benefit does nothing to help your bottom line (unless you are within a profession or market that requires a certain image).

Instead think about purchasing things that come along with ownership, investments, or other perks (tax breaks, equity, compound interest, items associated with deployment of built-up cash value, etc.).

But going back to the property portion, I believe it is important to look into investing into buying property (a house, rental property, or another variation) as it creates generational wealth and offers our descendants a better/decent start as they don't have to start off on square one. Now, I understand that home ownership or property ownership is not for everyone. But at least owning something (which you can calls your own and operate independently) creates opportunity and stability.

Investing & Money Management

After making substantial financial gains and working towards financial freedom, we must start also looking at investing a percentage of our money. I am not a financial adviser so take my ideas with a grain of salt and also do what is best for you. But what I will say is that managing and investing your money will bring about great results if you leverage it right and seek financial literacy for yourself (using reputable content, resources, and companies).

Investing may include real estate, index funds, launching a small business, flipping/reselling sneakers, or various methods of growing money. Investing can also include investing within yourself via certifications or obtaining (for example) an insurance license, CDL, barber license, real estate license, camera equipment (for content creation) or whatever you decide to invest within that fits your life. Just making sure you are investing a portion of your money to create more wealth and freedom/sovereignty.

In addition, making sure that you are managing your money is also extremely important. For instance, making sure you are paying your bills on time and not spending money on stuff you don't really need. Moreover, as men we must weigh our options regarding how to accurately spend our money. Which means knowing the difference between a financial asset and a depreciating liability. Investing and proper money management (saving, budgeting, and learning how finances work) is key.

Level Up, Don't Settle Down

Something that I see within some communities is a mindset and a willingness to simply settle sometimes. Ultimately this kind of mindset is not a masculine nor healthy mindset. I believe it is our job to continue the journey of leveling up (building financial security, creating generation wealth, breaking generational cycles, carry the torch for other generations, etc.).

What we ultimately see is brothers being discouraged and sometimes destroyed by a society as well as system that wants us to either rot internally or be oppressed externally (jail, prison, vices, addictions, or not being on our purpose). However when I think about the principles of leveling up it means to never settle for anything less than the full life that God prepared for us. Settling for an incomplete life is incorrect. Ultimately not settling for easy or the lifestyle that does not require discipline and hard work to achieve.

For example, I can honestly say college or entrepreneurship is not for everyone (I understand). But not attempting to leave a legacy, not learning a skill that you can use for a life, and not building your brand is inexcusable.

Being the fifteenth best at something simply because you did not try is not good enough (it doesn't matter the place/number but the investment in effort). Not seeking healing from past trauma because other generations did not is inexcusable. Heck even building relationships with someone that does not treat you right, but you are around them because you feel that is the best you can do is not good enough.

Being unhealthy and unmotivated, but not having the willingness to put in the work and not wanting to change your environment is inexcusable. Know yourself and know your worth…strive to be great not just average.

Be a Man of Your Word

Back in the day a man's word was more bounding and worthy than any contract or agreement. Ultimately, our elders understood that at the end of the day we only have our name and our word as men (and our word is bond). What we see now is that a lot of men do not allow their word to hold the same amount of weight (ultimately because many were not taught the principle of the important of self-respect).

A man should never agree to anything unless he is certain, and when appropriate if he must change his commitment, then it is always key to communicate that change as a man. Being a man of your word is not only verbal confirmation but a lifestyle and testament to your character.

It means being on time for work if you contractually agreed to work a set number of days/hours, it means being the person that you say you are privately and publicly. Now we all code switch sometimes and the work "you" is surely different from the at-home "you" but what I mean is knowing the difference. Which requires you to also understand the importance of not having a counterfeit persona or being two-faced. And it also means standing by your word (being as decisive and thorough as possible).

We as men must hold ourselves to a decent standard and a code of morals that individually govern our lives.

Building a Brotherhood

We as Black Men need brotherhood(s) throughout the continuous journey of life. Going back even to the Motherland and pre-colonized America, we have always had tribes. Within those tribes were generally male units that hunted, fished, educated, traded survival skills, and helped righteously define manhood for males in the village (present and future).

I am a huge proponent of thinking for myself and having decent time for solitude. And, I will always advocate for those measures and having that mindset. But also, life is about balance and finding a brotherhood (or creating one) based on common interest, goals, and ideas can be beneficial for personal growth.

Many examples of brotherhoods include male community organizations, college fraternities/campus organizations, church men's groups, gym workout squads, or even other community groups. All these opportunities offer the common opportunity for men to learn from one another, grow individually as well as collectively, and work towards a goal as a unit (group).

Understandably, not every organization or opportunity will be for you and will not align with your goals (that's okay). Finding your group will take time and measurable consideration. I also believe it is just as important to build a solid foundation and have mental/spiritual maturity so that you have a level of understanding about who you are as a man during the time that you decide to build such connections so that you will always have your individual ideas/morals.

But again, these organizations and groups are much needed particularly for Black Men.

One of the things that makes Black women smart (one of many reasons) is that sisters are more open to forming units for the greater good of other Black Women (and their collective community).

In the immature/younger stages (the word immature is not a diss but a form to show the level of growth), you see the bonding aspects within the context of that's my "girl/girl group." These business partnerships, friendships, and forming of tribes greatly helps them in every area of their life . On a healthy/mature spiritual level it creates generational wealth, a long list of resources/help for them, sisterhood, further identity, guidance, participation in something greater than them, bonds, and an unbreakable set of codes to live with daily (whether fully engaged or not) and a sense of protecting one another.

All thoughts aside, we as men need to create units and brotherhoods amongst ourselves to create further communities as well as promote standards of excellence.

I believe that we as men have slightly lost the idea of the collectivism and finding a tribe (but not to get confused with tribalism). During the days of my grandfather, the idea of mutual respect and collaboration amongst men in the community (or workplace, barbershop, neighborhood) was an important part of life.

Lately, I see countless instances where men are miserable or not living their full potential because we have lost the sense of the importance of brotherhood. We have gotten away from the masculine identity of having a brotherhood, and we either look at each other with an evil eye (read the book of Deuteronomy) or we simply do not find spaces to collaborate and build with one another.

Luckily, I do see it within certain spaces and several local platforms. But it is not nearly enough, and the brotherhoods must become more stronger as well as willing to engage/mentor the next generation of kings.

We need to get back into finding the right tribe and unit to constructively engage with as a collective group of men. That may include joining a pre-existing group or creating your own group based upon your goals, interest, or passions.

Take time to get involved with your community and look for ways to engage positive spaces with the goal of Black Male improvement.

Finding the One

Selecting the right life partner (the woman in which you will potentially spend the rest of your life with) is very important. Other than a few more important aspects of life (building a connection with God and finding purpose); finding the right one is one of the single most important decisions you will ever make as a man.

I can honestly say that I like many men have spent some of the younger years of my life without understanding the science of partner selection. I was looking for love with my eyes first, and at times with my eyes only. When in fact although attraction is extremely important, I will add that values and energy (**vibes**…do you all click with each other on multiple cylinders including morals, beliefs, and compatibility) are just as important.

Like I said, I really stress the importance of morals and compatibility. Ultimately, dating and marriage is just as much a political, financial, and cultural decision as it is a personal declaration/decision of love. First, particularly within my generation the idea of love has gotten at times flipped upside down. Maybe it has always been this way but with the invention of social media and reality TV; the destructive nature of dysfunction is broadcasted more than ever. And, dysfunction has almost become normalized within our communities and within "the culture."

True sustaining and successful relationships are built on faith as well as trust. If a relationship is built on anything else first (social media, aesthetics, or unreasonable expectations) it will be more stressful than enjoyable.

Now do not get me wrong, I know there are many great relationships that exist even across generations. I personally see it daily, and thankfully I personally know many happy young (and older) Black couples. I honestly say I know more good people in relationships then those that I would consider disastrous. However, I can also say that I know some horror stories that were a result of brothers not choosing wisely when it came to who they choose to build a relationship. In addition, I witness the outcomes that occurred because of being completely reckless or blinded by not thinking with a spiritually mature and decerning spirit (heart, mind, and soul).

When in a exclusive relationship y'all should be building each other up, making concrete plans for the future, growing as best friends while also filling in each other's gaps. Relationships should be built on God, growth, and encouragement. Not social media, hashtags stating "bae goals/relationship goals", trying to compete with one another on any level, and constant conflicting morals or belief systems.

I know that no relationship will be perfect, and the merging of two people into one joint partnership takes work. Yet, it should be built on positive things to elevate the relationship and not low vibrational things that will ultimately tear each other down (and ultimately make each other damaged goods for the next relationship).

So, I say to the fellas (especially my younger brothers) please slow down and stay on your purpose. Search but don't chase, and when you are searching use all your senses (and not just your eyes but your heart and all other common sense) to make the best decision. Take time to think about the qualities that you will want and need in a partner and map out the aspects of your life that needs self-improvement/development before the arrival of your queen and work on those things while you build, King!

But remember to always seek permission from God before you make any major decisions.

Break The Cycle

In certain sections of Black America, we have numerous cycles. A cycle of poverty, cycle of self-hatred, cycle of miseducation, or a cycle of pain. A bad cycle simply means a continuous and at times a generational continued pattern of negative life experiences/events. Although it is a heavy lift, we as Black Men are partially responsible for helping to break these negative cycles within our own lives and within the community.

For example, the cycle of fatherlessness can only be broken one man at a time. But we can change that aspect by being present within the lives of our own kids (no matter what challenges present themselves) and/or by being mentors/positive male role models within the community. Another example may be the cycle of poverty, which the cycle can be broken by smart financial decisions (budgeting, investing, and saving).

Another example may be the cycle of unresolved childhood or adult trauma. These traumas can affect anyone and can negatively affect generations to come if not accurately addressed.

Therefore, it is up to us to break negative cycles and generational barriers that present themselves. We as men must be the leaders and warriors that God created us to be in life. Therefore, as a Black Man please do your part within breaking the negative cycles in your personal life and in the community.

Take Charge, Take Responsibility

As a Black Man, we must continue to be the leaders of our community. A trend that I have continuously seen in our community is that the narrative is trying to shift Black Men from being leaders in the community, and thus not being responsible for the outcomes/issues of the community.

The narrative that we constantly see is the unconsciousness Black Man (one that does not care about the community…i.e., peep Young Thug's response to the Trayvon Martin killing), or the childish Black Man, the deadbeat dad, the heavily medicated careless Black Man, or any other negative narrative you can think of throughout the perceived culture of our community. We know these narratives are false. Yet propaganda combined with the promotion and glorification of these narratives have tried to slowly begin to make these false narratives a reality.

Now you may say that the agenda and narratives have nothing to do with us entirely. Partially, you may be right within some regards but as the topic eludes that if we as men do not take charge as well as take responsibility for our community then we cannot control what happens in our community. And, as a result the whole entire community loses because the community then becomes chaotic. We as men must continue to challenge ourselves to take responsibility of ourselves and our communities.

This pandemic has taught me a lot of things over the course of a year, one thing it taught me is that those that are lost or do not have a plan (either because of lack discipline and responsibility) will ultimately not live their life to the best of their abilities.

In addition, a man takes responsibility for his own actions. Whether good or bad, we must take responsibility for our own actions and the realities that we create for ourselves. A part of being a leader is leading oneself, leading and influencing others, and ultimately realizing that although responsibility can be a lot; it is our ultimate goal to not run from it but move towards it.

Find Your Purpose

In life one of man's greatest actions must be to ultimately find his purpose(s) in life. Every man has a purpose, but it is up to him to intentionally move towards that purpose in his life.

I believe that every man has been given a God given calling in life, but it is up to you as a man to actively channel the proper energy within yourself to discover then cultivate it. Everything happens for a reason and ultimately your purpose/destiny is tied within all aspects of your life.

For example, I grow up without my biological father in my life. It greatly hurt me and negatively affected me. And quite possibly played a role within some of the "less developed" areas of my life that would have been built with the help of a father. However, because he was not in my life, I have a continuous passion to help young Black Men. I have served in the role of mentor, coach, and have dedicated my life to helping countless young Black Men.

As a result, I found a part of my purpose which is to cultivate Black Men (of all ages) because of the void I had in my life. But also, it is because I was willing enough to submit to the will of GOD and not allow my pain to turn into my demise. I have begun the process of allowing my pain to heal so that I could find my purpose (turning pain into purpose). Again, it does not have to be pain or hurt that helps you discover your purpose. But you do have to be intentional.

I have been at my best as a man when I was intentional about my purpose. When I was distracted meaning letting ego get in the way, letting fear drive my actions, spending countless hours chasing distractions, or constantly wasting my youth on superficial/fading things is when I was not on my purpose. And no matter how much time that I wasted on unfulfilling things to fill the voids in my life, I ultimately felt empty and hopeless.

However when I am writing, mentoring, looking for ways to improve, and on my purpose; I feel my most powerful and I know I am at my best self. Not wasting time daydreaming about being my best self but putting in the work to be all that I can be in life.

Use Your Time Wisely

The martial artist Bruce Lee once said that "if you love life, then don't waste time because time is what life is made up of." These wise words are true as time is the most valuable measurable asset on planet earth. The resource is limited per person but universally unlimited within the context of the endless possibilities that can be created when time is used wisely.

We as Black Men particularly as young Black Men cannot wise time. And the excuse of youthful waste no longer applies to us as men since we have a mission that supersedes youthful ignorance or the idea that there will be a tomorrow which we can put off what we have purposefully planned for today. I once wrote "As uncomfortable as it sounds, life is way too short to not go for the things that you want and the things that will make you great. There is no tomorrow as the next day is simply a figment of our imagination until it actually comes into existence (and even then, it is not guaranteed for everyone). Don't use tomorrow as an excuse for why you choose to delay your God given calling. Choose today, don't just rely on tomorrow."

Within this short statement, I basically mean that life is meant to use the precious time that we have to make a difference and go for the things in life that will create a positive impact. Wasting time is like wasting the precious gifts that God has individually given you. Therefore, use time to produce greatness. Now you will still need time to relax, sleep, and enjoy life. But ultimately finding balance in every aspect of life is key. In life you must choose wisely and spend your time wisely.

Love Yourself

Loving yourself and knowing yourself is two of the hardest things to do in this world. It sounds simple, but the journey towards complete self-love, knowledge of oneself entirely, and inner peace is a constant journey (and at times a constant battle). Particularly for us as Black Men it can be particularly challenging. We live in a society that before we are even pushed out of our mother's womb this world seeks to destroy, distort, and break us down. And, once we are pushed out of our mother's womb, we are instantly subjected to attempts to be categorized, criticized, institutionalized, and marginalized.

Once we get of age, we are then miseducated, medicated, and indoctrinated. Then we are beaten down by society, made to feel like a fugitive or criminal in our own community, and ultimately many of us suffer in silence because we are either voiceless or too beaten down to speak up.

This is the plight for some brothers in America if we allow society to have its way. Now, I personally do not believe in blaming others for any flaws. But as the great Frederick Douglass said, "it's easier to build strong children than repair broken men." We live within a broken society that do not want us as Black Men to love and value oneself.

Therefore, I cannot stress the importance of self-love and self-care for us as Black Men. Ultimately, we must know that we are of value and that our life is of great substance. The journey to self-love is not easy, I still struggle with that idea daily. But the journey towards that mindset requires looking at yourself in the mirror (meaning internally) and being at peace with who you are as a man. Second, it requires getting on the journey of self-development and self-discovery. Last, it requires the power of knowing that you were created in the image of the Most High (and having a spiritual connection with the Almighty).

Loving yourself is something that you must do to be who God created you to be in life. God is perfect, and He would not create anything in vain or with distain. Therefore, learn to heal from your pain, find your purpose, and know you are worth it. As a man, you must know that you are worth it.

Look deeply within yourself and ask yourself this one question. Do you love…you? If the answer is not a definite yes, then take the necessary steps to learn to love yourself.

Don't Waste Your Seeds But Grow Them

Seeds are used to refer to a lot of things. From a biblical perspective it is associated with faith (for example having faith the size of a mustard seed) to the very idea of seeds representing the biological building blocks of life. Seeds also can be regarded as even the idea of life itself (people, ideas, goals, and the idea of growth). We have even heard the term used when referred to as Black Men in general, I mean we have all heard the statement that they tried to bury us, but they didn't know we were seeds.

As you can see that the idea of the seed is extremely important to us as men. Our seed which is our energy, essence, ideas, life's purpose, productive responsibility, and life force in general (basically all things that encompass us as men during our time on this earth).

In the Black Community (if we do not have a father, righteous male figure, or manhood organizations) we kind of just let manhood or the journey of Black Manhood happen.

Ultimately, we are not taught the importance of the "seed" and the greatness that is encompassed with it. In fact, we live in a society that promotes not only blood shed but also seed wasting/robbery. Again, our seed represents all aspects of life (mental, spiritual, linage, energy, physical manifestations, ideas, gifts, growth, and personal identity).

Yet, we waste our seed on negative things. We give our energy to negative things and waste our seeds on negative behaviors: ***petty beefs/interactions, wasteful social media use, squander precious time, not being on our purpose, low vibration activities, addictions, pornography, gluttonous behavior, jealousy, self-hate, hatred of other brothers, following propaganda-based trends that we are too blind to realize are manufactured to keep us at a low state in every area of life.***

All of these things keep us at a low vibration, and ultimately cause us to continue to waste the most precious gift that the Most High (Almighty GOD) has given us. And, if we are not careful can damage the very connection we have to the Most High.

Therefore as we close the first half of the book which has dealt with personal development, I say please guard your seeds. Know that the power of the Almighty is within you, and that it is your job as a man to manifest on earth the things that the Most High commanded. Continue to grow and elevate. Do not waste your time, energy, essence, ideas, will power, and life force on fruitless (and low vibration) things.

Part II (Community)

Now that we have taken solid steps towards being a steady foundation of manhood and personal responsibilities, it is time to discuss how we as Black Men must create, correct, and care for our community post-pandemic (and beyond)!

Circulating Black Wealth in the Black Community

One of the more important aspects that needs to be discussed is Black wealth creation and eventual circulation of wealth in our community.

Statistics state that the black dollar lasts in the Black community only a few hours. Whereas money in the Asian, Caucasian, and other non-Black communities stays in the Asian, Caucasian, and other non-Black community's money stays in their respective neighborhoods around fourteen to seventeen days on average (and due to certain community controls and ownerships some of the money never leaves which it ultimately remains circulating).

Thus, when you look at the conditions of some Black communities and the lack of ownership/representation, we began to see certain outcomes. Therefore, it is vital that we began to change the perspective of allowing money to instantly leave our community as soon as we get it (and not allow it to circulate).

Generally some experts point toward the formula which has previously been to get paid on Friday then pay bills, buy unnecessary items, buy food from non-black restaurants and grocery stores, stop by the barbershop (generally the only generally Black Owned business we patronize other than a restaurant or two), buy more unnecessary items (non-business related clothes, shoes, spending money at a bar, and a few other things) and by the time Friday afternoon rolls around the entire paycheck is gone and so is the money that could have been circulating in the Black Community.

Whereas if we made the intentional effort of buying from Black Owned Businesses, banking black, buying local, and navigating how to leverage our money so that our communities' benefit then we would instantly (almost over-night) begin to see economic and financial improvements in our communities. Which would also create changes in our social needs, decrease crime which is generally a direct result of lack of education or opportunity, improvements in our education system, increase in entrepreneurship, and increase the sense of sovereignty and self-sufficiency in our communities.

We have to support one another and began to circulate wealth within our communities to start seeing greater impact within the communities we love.

Supporting Black Owned Businesses & Banking Black

Speaking of circulating money within the Black Community translates perfectly into my next submission for your consideration which is supporting Black owned business (unapologetically) and banking with a Black owned bank (intentionally).

Unfortunately, within our communities we do not support our own businesses enough, and as a result our communities suffer unlike any other community. We see this more than ever in many aspects of the conditions of many communities, and the dependence upon jobs and/or systems that were never created for our success.

Moreover, we see the disconnect between the Black community and supporting Black owned businesses which has a negative effect on our communities. For example, Black owned business suffered the most financially during this pandemic (which is a result of lack of support/funding, and other factors related to Black owned businesses not receiving support on several levels).

And, the sad part is that Black owned businesses were already suffering before the pandemic. For example, Black people have over a trillion-dollar buying power (which would make us somewhere between the eight and thirteenth richest entity), but we only see about one to two percent of that spending power within our community.

Moreover, we see quite possibly the greatest case of how **not** supporting Black Owned Business is harming our communities and dismantling our historic and vital institutions. One example is the state of Black Owned Banks.

Black Owned Banks used to be one of the strongest institutions in Black America and offered us services as well as other financial resources. At the peak of Black Banking there were countless banks and community credit unions, which serviced our communities. However, we see a shocking reality that Black Owned Banks are decreasing at a rapid rate. Currently, there are roughly nineteen (19) Black Owned Banks left in America (which is an even greater decrease from the 48 that were left in 2001, and several hundred just a few decades ago).

Recently, we have seen the resurgence of the emphasis on supporting black owned institutions due to the impact of recent social justice events. Yet, the state of Black owned banks is sad especially within a country that has over fourteen million Black people in this country.

We must do a better job at banking/partnering with Black institutions, which is as simple as creating checking/saving accounts to support Black Owned banks as well as support their growth by patronizing the establishments (going to them for our general financial needs).

There is nothing wrong with having multiple banking accounts and places to keep your money. But not supporting any Black banks is the reason we see the shocking decline of Black banks which is truly unsettling. However, we can put in the work to change this fact and be the generation that brings about tangible solutions to several of our community issues. Therefore, I urge you to make a conscious effort to support Black owned businesses and banks.

Providing Mentorship to Young Black Men

At the end of the day, we must save our sons (when I say our sons, I mean young Black Men who are our sons either biologically or the sons from our collective communities).

If we can start to build up our young men, we can start to create substantial and everlasting change by mentoring, investing within, and supporting our youth. They need us more than ever, and we cannot let them grow up trying to be a man without understanding what a positive model of manhood encompasses. What we see right now in the media is not righteous or real manhood, but wickedness as well as propagated and corrupted images of Black masculinity.

In turn, young Black Men then see these images and are exposed to these narratives/experiences, which can cause confusion and a damaged understanding of manhood. As a result many young Black males do not have positive ideas or a productive understanding of personal black male image and a purposeful life. Thus, they may not be totally left to fail as several people have made it without a mentor. But it is very difficult and young Black Men are at a great disadvantage without positive male guidance and proper black male narratives as they try to navigate the complex journey of manhood.

Getting Involved with Community Efforts

Getting involved with community efforts is especially important for the growth and productiveness of our community. One of the best ways to build the community is by getting involved with existing programs or creating opportunities that make a positive impact.

There are many areas in which you can get involved and make a difference. Whether that is mentoring, education, health, environmental justice in urban areas, neighborhood revitalization, mental health, or any pressing issue in the community which you are passionate or can offer your support towards.

We talk a lot about redlining, racism, lack of voting, lack of education, lack of righteous manhood, etc.

But I ask the question…what can we do to fix it? I say this because we can talk about the issues (which bringing the injustices to light is important and is one of the first steps) but what are our next steps towards solutions. Therefore, I believe it is important to get involved with community efforts.

I am currently apart of several organizations serving as a mentor, and I also dedicate many of my weekends towards community efforts. In addition, I have lunched a lifestyle brand for young Black Men (with scholarships and other resources coming soon), and overall I have educated myself on community needs and looked for ways to lend support (whether with my time, finances, or external resources).

We as Black men cannot allow our communities to suffer and die. The aspect of sitting and watching while help in the community is constantly needed goes against the very will/plan of the Most-High. Therefore, we must find ways to constantly get involved and help our communities.

Again, everyone's strength may not be mentorship like mines, but simple things can go a long way to create change (cutting grass for elderly people in the community for free, offering free financial literacy classes online, creating a YouTube channel teaching various life skills, creating an organization or brand, serving as a mentor, volunteering your time with an organization that you are passionate about and whose mission is to uplift the Black community).

It is just as simple as finding ways to get involved.

Vote

I personally believe that voting is a very important aspect of elevating the community. Yet when I think about voting, I say making sure you vote in all elections is key. Especially, local and state elections. I believe that we have to make sure we are placing significant energy and effort within the elections that affect our lives as well as the lives of those in the community.

Moreover, we must do a better job at supporting the candidates that have our best intent in mind. And, if we know for sure that this particular "champion for our community" candidate does not exist, then we must do a better job at supporting and elevating someone qualified within our community to run for public office (that person may even be you).

In addition, one of the greatest impacts we can have on our community is voting in the elections that specifically affect our communities. Meaning voting for your local city councilor, the judge for the court of appeals, circuit judge, state AG, district judges/attorneys, and county commissioners. Also, the various bills, laws, and ordinances that affect our communities (bills regarding school superintendents, laws regarding education, laws regarding taxes or business licenses, and other rights we possess).

I always hear the elders stating "you cannot complain" if you did not vote. I will agree with this to an extent, but I would slightly change that phrase. You cannot complain if you did not vote for the elections that affect our community and you did not support the very elected officials that hold our best interest at heart. And, I would also add that if those people do not exist then we need to challenge, elevate, and support (politically, financially, and campaign support) a new wave of civil/public servants that can carry out our best interest.

Educate yourself on voting and the various policies, then find ways to make substantial change in your community. And also separately, please learn your local and state laws. It is very important for us as men to educate ourselves on the laws, codes, and information that governs our communities. That includes knowing your rights if pull over by law enforcement to knowing the proper laws that exist to keep your community functioning.

Level Up, Don't Settle Down (Part II)

You have countless men living a life that is either unfulfilled or greatly lacking because they decided to settle down, and not level up. When I mean level up and not settling down, it has nothing to do with dating. But I am referring to living a life of attempting to be the absolute best and going for the things that you want in life.

I honestly refuse to settle below the bar and live a mediocre life. God did not intent for us to live a low-vibrating and basic life, but to live abundantly and fruitfully. Never settling down does not mean never getting married or not being satisfied with life (both are very important). For me, never settling down means never being okay with giving half-effort or settling below your abilities.

I absolutely love the Roommates Podcast, and one of the hosts talks a lot about instead of simply daydreaming about the future actually begin the process of actually envisioning and then creating the life you want to live.

The host explains visualizing yourself within the next 10, 20, or 30 years. Envision the car you want to drive, the kids you want, the house you want, the relationships (personal and professional) you want, the physique you desire, your future wife, and everything other aspect of life. Then, once you have envisioned those things then map out the necessary steps needed to achieve those goals.

For example, a prime example of envision plus leveling up and not settling down is having body goals. If you want the best physique possible or a generally more muscular frame, then instead of settling down for less than you know you can achieve (eating little Debbie cakes instead of fruit/vegetables, being a couch potato instead of getting up and going to the gym, not getting enough sleep or water), you should be pushing yourself to level up to the next level of the most optimal "you" possible.

That's basically what never settling down means, which is not settling for below your means out of fear or laziness. And it is important that the community learns the same values.

Leadership in the Community

I have stated and restated this information throughout this book, but it is vital for us as Black Men to challenge as well as continuously lead the community. Being a leader and a man is not a one-off event or something that we can do on a part-time basis. Being a strong Black Man means being mentally, spiritually, and physically strong while also elevating the community. It is a very hefty task, but it is something that we were created to do.

Imagine an entire group or generation of Black Men that are working to create the change that is much needed in our communities. I heard this quote once and it changed my life which is that it "starts and ends with the man."

We cannot allow the destruction and hurt within our communities to continuously happen. We must challenge the community to be better, and then lead the efforts to bring about the evolution. After every great struggle or journey there has always been something called a renaissance era. Meaning a revival or renewal of a community, culture, or idea.

After this time period that we have had throughout the community it is time for us as Black Men to have a renaissance where we refocus our attention on the things that brought us the blocks of success we had in the community (strong black male images/narratives, self-love, knowledge of self, building our communities, critical thought, and detailed culture).

We cannot let another year, or another era go by without us taking control of our narrative and the influence on direct pathways towards healing and the overall health (mental, financial, social, educational, political, economic, and other aspects) of the community.

I personally think that if we do not seize this opportunity that God has given us (which in some regards has been a time to refocus, shift, and strategize) then we may never get a chance like this ever again to make a collective substantial shift or change in our community. I have only said this once within this book, but it is the most important. We must figure out the issues and work to fix them.

Learning & Teaching Love of Self

You cannot fully and properly love anyone else (or even the community) before you fully accept and love yourself. This is one of the more complex aspects as many Black men have never been taught to understand the importance of self-reflection and self-love. There are few avenues, narratives, or outlets to support the Black man in America regarding knowledge of self and self-love/respect.

That is why organizations and programs like The Cave of Adullam (Yunion, Inc.) and many other programs for young black men are incredible. Understanding the root of the pain of the past or simply learning knowledge of self is important because it will eventually bring inner peace to you as a person.

Therefore, we as Black Men must learn how to heal and continuously be on the path towards being whole as a person. Moreover, we must create narratives for others to see a path towards growing into their best selves through this method of healing and wisdom. Overall, learning to love yourself means being able to release your fears, scarcity mindsets, and learning to be the most authentic possible.

I know this is extremely hard work because I am still on the journey towards complete freedom and being my best-self. However, once you begin that path you will see that things within your life will change and your energy will be different. The principle of teaching self-love to our communities is vital.

Love The Community

You honestly must have a true love for the community to fully be committed to seeing it succeed. I genuinely and truthfully mean that statement.

The reason why I want to see us win so bad is because I love our community, and I know the true challenges that we face daily. However, I know that we can also be the change that we want to see. It starts and ends with us. According to the Word, we are the rightful overseers and operators of this Earth which God created for us. It is our life's purpose and a part of our mission as men to create and restore. Meaning creation which is physical creation of life but also bringing to life the ideas and opportunities that will create improvements (basically giving physical life to the spiritual gifts/ideas God gave you and helping others cultivate their gifts).

The second portion of the purpose of man and the significance it has related to loving the community is the goal to restore it to its optimal state. A man is meant to create and restore. But a man will ultimately neglect the very things he does not love or appreciate (and ultimately despises). Therefore by loving the community, we understand the issues within it and seek to make the effort to fix those issues.

Abundance Mindset

Having an abundance mindset is truly key to success in many aspects of life (I would go as far to say all aspects of life). The opposite of an abundance mindset is a scarcity mindset which I see constantly from men within the areas of business, relationships, money, opportunities, etc.

Having a scarcity mindset significantly hurts the quality of your life and robs you of the fullness (or fulfillment) of the promises that the Most High has for your life. Scarcity is simply having a fear of outcomes, scared of life or what others think, having a mindset of lack, not living life to the fullest, and having a counterfeit persona which is due to a lack of true confidence and a weak connection to the Almighty (which we were created in His image/likeness).

On the other hand, having an abundance mindset means being able to create freely, not being fearful of things that you cannot control, not having a fear of rejection, being open to new opportunities, being financially stable by making good decisions, being able to be whole, being emotionally healthy, and being spiritually mature.

Scarcity says that I "cannot", or I will never get that opportunity, I'm not smart enough, I'm not tall enough, she will reject me, I can't achieve that, I'm not sharing the spotlight, etc.

Whereas with abundance mindset, you realize that ultimately what is for you will be for YOU.

Moreover, you will realize that every thought you have (positive or negative) and every decision you make has a specific outcome. You will begin to live a life of purpose, and in return you will begin to constantly be on your purpose. That is the abundance mindset, which is being your best self and living life abundantly (and freely).

Collectivism

Collectivism is ultimately defined as focusing on the collective and the overall collective good of others. Within this entire book, I have preached the importance of four things: self-improvement, sovereignty, collectivism, and abundance. For Black Men (and the community) to thrive it takes us doing the work to be all that we can be because at the end of the day…we are all we got. It is important to focus on individual health, happiness, and success (these keys are important to a full and functional life). Yet we must also begin to take into account the importance of building the best community possible.

The principles accomplished in this book offer a small checklist of actions that can be taken to achieve individual success and collective success for the community. If we as an entire community decided to have a collective mindset, we could not only be our ancestor's wildest dreams, but also bring our own individual and collective dreams into reality. We do this by creating for ourselves and creating with others in mind. Begin to process the mindset of abundance and then construct the goals associated with collectivism, and we can truly be powerful.

Closing Words

We as Black Men have a job that no one else on Earth has which encompasses many things addressed in this book, and probably so much more. Like stated earlier, it is a heavy task but it is a task that we can complete. So, I ask you this question. Will you fight hard for the freedom of yourself and your community? Or do you enjoy the emptiness that comes from a lack of impact?

I have felt that emptiness when I was not using the gifts and information that God gave me to change the outcomes around me. I can attest to the pain, suffering, hurt, and misguidance of many in our communities (and again even ourselves in some context).

Mr. Jason Wilson talks about "fighting for freedom and breaking from emotional incarceration" in his best-selling book. That is what being a man is about…learning to navigate the world while also fighting to bring about freedom and peace (for yourself and others).

We have had the unprecedented experience of not simply being quarantined for the sake of a virus but also given the opportunity to remove ourselves from toxic environments, social circles, and social media platforms. This period of reflection was presented to us, so that we could reset ourselves for the long journey ahead of us. We cannot allow this time and this moment to be wasted or taken for granted.

But use the time that was given effectively and (and if you are reading this and we are already out of the pandemic then starting today) proceed to build yourself and then build the community.

Black Man… you are great and we can succeed. Learn to lead by example, learn to love yourself, learn to connect with the Most High, and be the change that you want to see.

Mungu Ni Mkuu (God Is Great)!

Author's Note/What Did You Think of the Book?

First, thank you for purchasing a copy of the book "The Black Man's Guide to Self-Improvement Post-Pandemic." You could have selected any book, so I greatly appreciate the support.

Please let me know what you thought of the book by leaving an honest review on Amazon.com. By leaving a review on Amazon, it helps me grow as a writer and it spreads the reach of the book on the website as well. In addition, please also leave a review on Goodreads.com if you are on the platform.

This book has been almost two years in the making, so again I say thank you for supporting our efforts in discussing tangible solutions regarding Black Male self-improvement and community building.

It has been an amazing experience writing this book, and I already look forward to the next one. To stay connected checked our website, heisbham.com

We are also on YouTube (@Heisbham)!

About The Author

D. Forte is a community servant leader and education advocate. He is the creator of HE IS B'ham which is a lifestyle brand for young Black Men to shift the narrative surrounding our personal image and provide information on self-improvement to men of all ages. He holds degrees in Black Studies and criminal justice. He is currently pursuing his master's degree in public administration.